PRIMARY SOURCES TEACHING KIT

The Westward Movement

by Karen Baicker

SCHOLASTIC
PROFESSIONAL BOOKS

New York • Toronto • London • Auckland • Sydney
Mexico City • New Delhi • Hong Kong • Buenos Aires

for Virginia Dooley and Sarah Longhi

Edited by Sean Price
Picture research by Dwayne Howard
Cover design by Norma Ortiz
Interior design and illustrations by Melinda Belter
ISBN 0-590-37844-9

1 2 3 4 5 6 7 8 9 10   40   09 08 07 06 05 04 03 02

Contents

INTRODUCTION

Using Primary Sources in the Classroom

You may have textbooks in your classroom that describe the Westward Movement—the excitement and hardships, and life on the frontier. But nothing makes the period come alive for students more than to read the real words of someone traveling on the wagon train or to see a photograph of a sod-house schoolroom.

Primary sources offer a wealth of other benefits to your students as well. Textbooks often present a single interpretation of events; primary sources compel the reader to supply his or her own interpretation. A thoughtful analysis of primary sources requires both basic and advanced critical thinking skills: classifying documents, determining point of view, evaluating bias, comparing and contrasting, and reading for detail.

Primary sources can also help students recognize that the artifacts of our contemporary lives—a ticket stub, a school report card, a yearbook—may one day be fodder for future historians.

One of the most important steps in teaching history is to help students understand the difference between primary and secondary sources. Share the chart below to demonstrate the categories to your class.

MATERIAL	DEFINITION	EXAMPLES
Primary Sources	Documents created during or immediately following the event they describe, by people who had firsthand knowledge of the event	Letters, diaries, photographs, artifacts, newspaper articles, paintings
Secondary Sources	Documents created by people who were not present at the event they occurred	History books, biographies, newspaper articles

Keep a folder handy with copies of the primary source evaluation form on page 15. Encourage students to complete the reproducible as they study each document in the book. Eventually, this kind of analysis will be automatic for your students as they encounter primary sources in their future studies.

Using the Internet to Find Primary Sources

The Internet can be an amazing tool for finding primary sources. Just remind your students that extra care has to be taken in verifying that the source is reliable. Here are a few outstanding sites for using primary sources in the classroom:

Library of Congress: **http://www.loc.gov**

National Archives Records Administration: **http://www.nara.gov**

Internet Archive of Texts and Documents: **http://history.hanover.edu/texts.htm**

The Making of America: **http://moa.umdl.umich.edu**

The End of the Oregon Trail: **http://www.endoftheoregontrail.org**

Ask your students to find other great sites for primary sources and create their own list. Keep a running list handy, posted near a computer terminal.

Background on the Westward Movement (1775–1896)

The history of the United States has often been presented as one of westward movement. From the time of the explorers sailing west from Europe and reaching our shores, through the colonies, to the Mississippi, and beyond to Oregon and California, the past has been written by our westward-shifting frontiers.

More recently, increased cultural awareness has altered this perspective. The Native Americans who had lived on the land for thousands of years were not moving westward—at least not voluntarily. Nor was their world "expanding," another word frequently used to describe the westward movement. In fact, the land they knew and their resources were contracting.

Nonetheless, the events and images from this time period remain a powerful and important part of our history, and of our common culture. Elicit adjectives used to describe the pioneers—industrious, determined, brave, resourceful—and you will note characteristics still central to our national identity.

The westward movement is populated with colorful, legendary figures, including Daniel Boone, Davy Crockett, Wild Bill Cody, Annie Oakley, and fearless explorers such as Meriwether Lewis and William Clark. But the primary sources of ordinary people, their diaries and letters and photographs, tell an equally compelling story.

About This Book

The documents that follow provide snapshots into an exciting and inspiring era. They include a variety of primary source texts and images from the period 1775 to 1896. This collection of sources—from early portrait photographs to diary entries and newspaper articles—offers your students new ways to learn more about the Westward Movement, and prompts them to look for more eyewitness accounts from the people who were there.

Your students will benefit most from working with these documents when you help to set a context and engage them with critical viewing and thinking activities. Students can prepare for a discussion about any of the documents in this collection by studying them and completing the student reproducible Evaluate That Document! (page 15). This primary source evaluation form guides students to identify important document characteristics and pose questions prior to class discussion. Feel free to reproduce this form as you need it.

The Teaching Notes section provides background information and teaching suggestions for each document. Reproducible pages for the activity suggestions can be found at the back of the book.

Some documents, such as the Louisiana Purchase Treaty (page 16), feature text that is difficult to read. For these, as well as for lengthy documents, we have included typeset selections along with the original. This way, students can explore the text as an actual, physical document, and also understand the contents. In some cases, when original documents were not available, we have typeset the text, as in Chief Joseph's speech (page 40).

Time Line of the Westward Movement

(1775–1896)

1775	Daniel Boone opens the Wilderness Road to Kentucky
1803	The Louisiana Purchase: U.S. buys Louisiana Territory from France for $15 million
1804–1806	The Lewis and Clark Expedition maps territory from Missouri to California
1807	The Clermont, Robert Fulton's steamboat, makes its first run from New York City to Albany, New York
1812	The United States declares war on Britain
	The Erie Canal opens in New York
1830	The Indian Removal Act is passed
1830–1842	The Cherokee Indians are forced to move to Oklahoma via "The Trail of Tears"
1843	The first group of wagoneers travels the Oregon Trail
1845	The term "manifest destiny" is first used to justify westward expansion
1847	Mormons follow Brigham Young to Utah
1848	Gold nuggets are discovered at Sutter's Mill in California; beginning of Gold Rush
1860	The Pony Express carries mail from Missouri to California in 10 days
1861	The Transcontinental telegraph line is completed
1862	The Homestead Act is created
1869	The Transcontinental Railroad is completed
1873	Barbed wire is introduced
1876	Custer is killed at the Battle of Little Bighorn in Montana
1887	Railroads create time zones to coordinate train schedules
1896	Gold is discovered in Klondike, Alaska

Scholastic Professional Books

TEACHING NOTES

The Louisiana Purchase Treaty: 1803

Use with pages 16–17.

BACKGROUND

In 1803, Louisiana was controlled by France, under the leadership of the new French emperor, Napoleon. Napoleon needed cash to fight wars in Europe, so he struck what became known as one of the greatest real estate deals in history with the United States President, Thomas Jefferson.

The signing of the Louisiana Purchase added 828,000 square miles of territory to the United States, almost doubling the size of the country for $15 million, or about 3 cents an acre. It also brought the nation back from the brink of war with Spain and France.

TEACHING SUGGESTIONS

❋ Distribute copies of Evaluate That Document! (page 15) to help students analyze the Louisiana Purchase. Discuss the idea that a treaty—though just a piece of paper with writing on it—can alter the course of history. Explain that major international agreements are still made the same way, with leaders sitting around a table and hammering out an agreement.

❋ To help students grasp the geographic scope of the Louisiana Purchase, distribute the Westward Movement Map (page 45). Students should recognize that the treaty ceded all of the land between the Mississippi River and the Rocky Mountains to the United States. Ask students to color in the United States territories before and after the Louisiana Purchase (encourage them to use a color key).

❋ Discuss the fact that the issues of land and territory have been the cause of many wars. Help students examine the causes and effects of the Louisiana Purchase. Ask students to consider how treaties may prevent wars.

The Lewis and Clark Expedition: 1804-1806

Use with pages 18–20.

BACKGROUND

Following the Louisiana Purchase, President Thomas Jefferson authorized a major expedition to explore the Louisiana territory. Meriwether Lewis and William Clark led that expedition, and Jefferson charged them with making maps, keeping records of what they saw, and describing the Indians they met along the way.

The documents shown here include a photograph of their leatherbound journals; an excerpt from The Journals of the Expedition under the Command of Captains Lewis and Clark; *a buffalo robe the explorers sent back to Jefferson and a list of other artifacts; and some sketches from their journals. The buffalo robe is from a Mandan man, who had painted it with illustrations of a battle of the Mandans and Hidatsas against the Lakotas and the Arikaras. Jefferson displayed the robe at Monticello and it now hangs at Harvard's Peabody Museum.*

TEACHING SUGGESTIONS

❋ Distribute copies of Evaluate That Document! for students to use as they consider the primary sources representing the expedition of Lewis and Clark on pages 18–20.

❋ Have students find the rivers described in the excerpt on page 18. Ask why McNeal might have been "exultant."

❋ Ask students to write their own journal entry of an imaginary expedition, modeling it on the journal excerpt on page 18 and using the journal reproducible on page 49.

❋ Ask students to consider the buffalo robe and list on page 19. Why do they think Lewis and Clark chose those objects to send to President Jefferson? What do they think he learned from them?

❋ Note that recently there has been speculation about the authenticity of the buffalo robe. Ask students to research what the latest analysis suggests.

❋ Ask students to draw an illustration of a common natural object, describing it as if they had not seen it before, in the manner of the fish shown on page 20.

The Crockett Almanac: 1841

Use with page 21.

BACKGROUND

The larger document is from the cover of The Crockett Almanac *of 1841. The small reproduction is a woodcut from Davy Crockett's 1837* Almanack of Wild Sports in the West, *and is entitled* A Desperate Contest with a Great Black Bear. *Students may be familiar with the Davy Crockett of legend. In reality, Davy Crockett was a pioneer who served in the Tennessee legislature and the United States Congress. He died in Texas defending the Alamo against Mexico in 1836, just before the interior illustration was published. The almanacs he published contributed to the folklore of the wild American West.*

TEACHING SUGGESTIONS

✺ Have students examine these prints and discuss what they reveal about life in the West. Distribute copies of Evaluate That Document! (page 15) to help students analyze these documents.

✺ Provide a copy of the lyrics to "The Ballad of Davy Crockett." (You can find the lyrics online at Info Please: **http://www.infoplease.com /askeds/5-4-01askeds.html**.) Ask students to determine which parts of the song—and the legends—were most likely true.

✺ Note that the banner heading of the 1841 almanac cover reads "Go Ahead!!" Ask students what they think this motto refers to. Ask them to examine the "Tussel with a Bear" illustration. Who appears to be winning? How is that same struggle depicted differently in the other illustration?

✺ Explore the legends of Daniel Boone, another colorful character from the time. Daniel Boone was one of the early pioneers, who forged the Wilderness Road through Kentucky in 1775. This route is shown on the Westward Movement Map on page 45. Some historians mark Boone's trailblazing as the beginning of the Westward Movement.

On the Trail: 1847–1849

Use with pages 22–24.

BACKGROUND

The Oregon Trail is the most famous of the trails pioneers carved out of the rugged landscape of the West. The trail began at Independence, Missouri (the jumping-off point), and followed the south bank of the Platte River, continued West through Nebraska, into Wyoming, and through the Rocky Mountains all the way to Oregon. The route was over 2,000 miles long.

Settlers were encouraged to take the trip by offers of free land from the United States government. More than 350,000 people made the arduous trip, one filled with hardship and peril, as evidenced in the diary excerpts on pages 24–25.

The constitution shown on page 23 is a document written by the leaders of a wagon train. Groups often elected leaders to write such rules of conduct during the first weeks on the trail.

TEACHING SUGGESTIONS

✺ Distribute copies of Evaluate That Document! (page 15) for students to use as they analyze the various documents representing the pioneer experience on the Oregon Trail.

✺ Encourage students to use the KWL chart on page 44 to examine their prior knowledge and set goals to research the Oregon Trail.

✺ Have students look at the photograph showing the interior of a covered wagon, packed for the journey, on page 23. Encourage students to do research and create a list of supplies needed for the six-month trip to Oregon.

✺ Ask students to read the constitution on page 22. Have them imagine that they are setting out on a journey. What sort of constitution would they write to govern themselves and their fellow travelers?

✺ Students can use the game cards on page 46 to explore some of the obstacles that the pioneers encountered.

The Gold Rush: 1849

Use with pages 25–26.

BACKGROUND

Soon there was another strong lure out West—the discovery of gold by John Marshall at Sutter's Mill in 1848. In the years that followed, thousands of people clamored to reach California from all over the world. It launched one of the greatest migrations of people in American history. In one single year, 1849, the population of California increased from 20,000 to more than 100,000.

The trip was difficult, the camps were dangerous, and living conditions were incredibly expensive and occasionally violent. Some struck it rich. For many, however, the promises of wealth did not pan out.

TEACHING SUGGESTIONS

☀ Distribute the Evaluate That Document! (page 15). The reproducible and discuss how the different types of documents shown on pages 25–26 provide different views of the Gold Rush.

☀ Review the advertisements and ask students to consider the expectations and hopes that might be raised by them. Were the ads accurate? What do they demonstrate about the emotional climate at the time?

☀ Based on the photograph on page 25, what can students infer about what panning for gold was like? Point out the Chinese workers and provide some background about the role of Chinese immigrants in the Gold Rush. Also point out that there were very few women who went to California during the Gold Rush, and explain that their role was often to serve the miners.

☀ Help students interpret the cartoon on page 27. The illustration, created by Nathaniel Currier, is titled "The Way They Go to California." In it, he depicts imaginative ways that desperate gold-seekers might get to California. After your discussion, investigate the actual ways people could get to California at the time.

Horse Tracks at Ordinary Speed: 1863

Use with page 27.

BACKGROUND

The wood engraving of horse tracks on page 28 comes from a how-to guide for pioneers written by Randolph B. Marcy, called The Prairie Traveler, a Hand-Book for Overland Expeditions *(the cover appears on this page, as well). The guide featured maps and detailed descriptions of the major overland routes between Mississippi and the Pacific Ocean. It included such tips as how to best pack a wagon and what to do in case of snakebite. This chart shows how a traveler can interpret a horse's hoof prints to determine the speed and type of horse.*

TEACHING SUGGESTIONS

☀ Distribute copies of Evaluate That Document! and ask students what type of information the horse-tracks chart gives about life in the mid 1800s.

☀ Use the chart as a springboard to discuss what limited information the pioneers were working with, and how they used the information of those who had passed before them to try to make their own journey successful.

☀ The chart can be used as a math connection. Ask students to calculate roughly how many feet are shown in each column of the chart.

☀ What can a reader imply about Marcy's view of "Indians" and the interaction he expects his readers might have with them?

The Pony Express: 1860

Use with page 28.

BACKGROUND

Although the Pony Express is legendary, it was in existence for only 19 months. In March, 1860, the first rider took off on horse from St. Joseph, Missouri, with 49 letters and a newspaper. Using a rider-relay system, the mail reached Sacramento just 10 days later, faster than with any system previously used.

The Pony Express captured people's imaginations and brought news from the "Golden State" of California closer. However, the advent of the telegraph (page 29) soon put the Pony Express out of business.

TEACHING SUGGESTIONS

❁ Have students evaluate the Pony Express flyer using the Evaluate That Document! form.

❁ Ask students to find Leavenworth, Kansas, and Sacramento, California, on a map and use the map key to measure the distance between the two cities (almost 2,000 miles). Students can compare the rates for sending mail from the time of the Pony Express to today's express rates. They can also compare mail delivery time between 1860 and today by sending a letter to another place about 2,000 miles away and tracking how long it takes to get there.

❁ Have students compare the Pony Express flyer to advertisements for a carrier today, such as Federal Express or the United States Postal Service.

❁ Pose this question: If each rider covered about 200 miles a day for ten days and changed horses every 10 miles, how many horses would a rider use in 10 days?

❁ Ask students what might be meant by the expression "Clear the Track" on the poster.

Completion of The Overland Telegraph: 1861

Use with page 29.

BACKGROUND

The documents on this page show a key development in the history of communication. The telegraph was invented in 1844 by Samuel F. B. Morse, and the photographs show the tape from the first message sent over telegraphic wires—from Washington, D.C., to Baltimore. The message reads "What hath God wrought?" The words are encoded in dots and dashes embossed into the long tape by signals from electrical impulses.

The 1861 excerpt from The New York Times *highlights the completion of the Overland Telegraph line, from New York to San Francisco. This accomplishment enabled the invention to be used to communicate across the country. It effectively put the Pony Express (see page 28) out of business.*

TEACHING SUGGESTIONS

❁ Ask students to read *The New York Times* article excerpt on page 29 and fill in an Evaluate That Document! form (page 15) to examine this primary source more closely.

❁ Have students examine the Morse code tape alphabet display (page 29) and the Crack the Code reproducible (page 47) to familiarize themselves with the form of Morse code. Let students practice sending their own Morse code messages on paper.

❁ Ask students to consider why Morse might have chosen the words "What hath God wrought?" What message might they have chosen for the first transcontinental communication?

❁ Ask students to list some other inventions that have changed the way people communicate. Encourage them to do research to learn more about them.

❁ Show students a simple way that they can practice sending a classmate a telegraph with Morse code. (See the S-O-S! directions on Crack the Code.)

Growth of the Railroad: 1860s

Use with pages 30–32.

BACKGROUND

In 1862, President Abraham Lincoln signed a bill authorizing the construction of a transcontinental railroad. In 1863, two companies began building the railroad—one from Sacramento, California, going east and one from Omaha, Nebraska, heading west.

The task was monumental and made a huge impact on the surrounding environment and the people involved. The railroad construction blasted tunnels through mountains, while new rails and bridges interrupted animal habitats. The lands of Native Americans were violated, and buffalo were killed off. Many people suffered backbreaking toil, including Chinese and Irish laborers.

However, six years later, in 1869, the two lines met in a much-celebrated moment at Promontory, Utah. The joining of the two long lines of track was historic, symbolic, and an incredible development in transportation. The amount of time for the overland journey was reduced from five months to eight days.

TEACHING SUGGESTIONS

- Ask students to explore why the completion of the railroad was such an historic moment. Using the Evaluate That Document! form (page 15), examine the photograph on page 31 for nuances. What do the expressions of different people reveal?

- Read the words that were engraved on the golden spike that was driven into the ground to unite the two rails. (Note: The spike that is shown on page 31 was later removed for posterity.) Encourage a discussion of the significance of the inscription. Ask students to create their own text for the golden spike.

- When the final spike was hammered in, it triggered a telegraph signal that let the country know the mission was complete. The signal over the wire read, "DONE!" Explore the ways that communication and transportation were uniting the country in that single moment.

- Point out that the transcontinental railroad did not happen overnight. Train travel existed before, and railroads were gradually spreading out, heading west. Have students look at a U.S. map to compare the distances covered and times indicated between the timetable on page 30 and the advertisement on page 32. Discuss how train travel changed in one decade.

American Progress: 1873

Use with page 33.

BACKGROUND

The painting shown is one of the most commonly used images to depict the Westward Movement. George Crofutt was a publisher of travel guidebooks, and he commissioned John Gast to create a painting to be used as an illustration for his Western guides. He dictated to Gast the specific elements to incorporate in the painting. After it was completed, he made thousands of prints for the readers of his travel series.

The painting, American Progress, *symbolizes the many aspects of the Westward Movement, including what became known as* manifest destiny. *The floating figure, pointing westward, suggests the inevitability of America's expansion.*

TEACHING SUGGESTIONS

- Have students search for symbolism in the painting on page 33. Which elements depict transportation? Communication? Distribute Evaluate That Document! to help students analyze this painting.

- Ask students to make a sketch for a painting called *American Progress Today.* What would they show?

- Encourage students to look closely at the people depicted in the painting. What can they say about the artist's views toward men and women, based on the painting?

- Explore the concept of *manifest destiny.* Have students research when the term came about and what attitudes it reflected about the Westward Movement.

Glidden's Barbed Wire Patent: 1874

Use with page 34.

BACKGROUND

Barbed wire is an example of a seemingly minor invention—a mere twist of metal, it might appear—that changed the landscape of life in the West. Before the invention of barbed wire, fencing was extremely problematic. Animals easily broke plain wire fences. Wooden fences were expensive and lumber was in scarce supply (thus the sod houses on farms).

In the 1870s, various versions of barbed wire emerged and competed for patents. The most successful of these was Joseph Glidden's, shown on page 34. He also developed machinery to mass-produce the wire, adding to its success and popularity.

No longer did cattle roam freely and cowboys lead cattle drives. Farms and other property became more private, resources were less available for common use, and range wars were waged. Many Native American groups, used to nomadic lifestyles, were negatively affected. In fact, they called barbed wire "the Devil's rope." Nostalgia for the open lands developed almost immediately, captured in Cole Porter's song "Don't Fence Me In."

TEACHING SUGGESTIONS

❋ Ask students to discuss why the patent itself is considered a primary source. Distribute Evaluate That Document! (page 15) to aid students in their analysis.

❋ Divide the class into groups representing different populations' perspectives—those of Native Americans, farmers, cowboys, and wire manufacturers. Ask each group to write a paragraph describing the new invention from their point of view.

❋ Have students discuss Glidden's purpose in designing the fence. According to Glidden's patent application, what is the purpose of his invention? Direct students' attention to the third paragraph, which describes the purpose and advantages of the barbed wire design.

❋ Distribute the words to Cole Porter's song "Don't Fence Me In." Ask students to discuss the perspective conveyed by the song. Lyrics for this song, as well as other information about Cole Porter, can be found online at **http://www.coleporter.org**.

❋ Ask students to compare Glidden's invention with others they've seen in this collection: the railroad and the telegraph. Ask them to consider the impact of these inventions on our lives today.

Life on the Frontier— Pioneers and Cowboys: Late 1800s

Use with pages 35–37.

BACKGROUND

The montage of photographs on pages 35–37 offer several views of life for cowboys and pioneers of the American West.

The photographs were taken in the late 1800s. The houses were generally built out of the material most readily available—earth. Strips of sod were chopped into three-foot lengths and stacked in rows, like bricks. The houses that have wooden doors and glass windows reveal that the families living in them were among the more prosperous. The roofs of sod houses were covered with hay or brush, but most of them leaked when it rained.

Although the cowboys worked long, hard days, the photographs also reveal that they had fun, and carried with them a sense of pride.

TEACHING SUGGESTIONS

❋ Ask students to evaluate these photographs using the Evaluate That Document! form.

❋ Point out that photography was a relatively new invention in the late 1800s and equipment was rare, expensive, and complicated to set up. Ask students why this might account for the formal poses of the subjects.

❋ Ask students to write their own captions for one of the photographs shown on page 35. Let them know that the bottom photograph shows a woman being handed the deed for her new property.

❋ Explore the romantic notion of cowboys and the images portrayed in film and literature. Encourage students to discuss why cowboys captured such a place in America's imagination. Have them look at the photograph at the top of page 36. How does it reflect the image of the cowboy in American culture?

✹ What do the photographs on page 37 show about the life of a cowboy?

The Wild West: 1898

Use with pages 38–39.

BACKGROUND

Perhaps nothing conveyed the exciting appeal of the Wild West better than Buffalo Bill's Wild West show, organized by William Cody in 1883 and performed for 30 years. The show featured bucking broncos, lassoing cowboys, and an international exhibition called the Congress of Rough Riders of the World.

The performers demonstrated roping, shooting, and riding skills, and portrayed tales of cowboys, Indians, the Pony Express, hunters, and cavalry scouts. These often-exaggerated portraits contributed to the romantic myth of life in the American West.

Performers included Annie Oakley, Buck Taylor, and even the Sioux chief, Sitting Bull (although he found it demeaning and quit after one season).

TEACHING SUGGESTIONS

✹ Ask students to discuss the point of view toward the American West conveyed by the poster on pages 38–39. Distribute the Evaluate That Document! form (page 15) to help students prepare for the discussion.

✹ Let students know that Chief Sitting Bull declined to participate in the show after one season. Ask students to study the document for clues about why Sitting Bull might have felt that way.

✹ Ask students to try to determine how Native Americans were portrayed in these shows.

✹ Have students create their own posters or tickets for the Wild West show.

Chief Joseph's Surrender Speech: 1877

Use with page 40.

BACKGROUND

Chief Joseph was the leader of the Nez Percé Indians who lived in the Wallowa Valley (in present-day Oregon, Idaho, and Washington). In the early 1870s, the Nez Percé were engaged in a losing battle against the United States Army for their land. Chief Joseph was their leader, and he began to realize that they could not continue to fight. However, he did not want to surrender. He led a march to Canada in 1877. The tribe successfully crossed the rugged terrain of Idaho and Montana (more than 1,000 miles) fighting off entanglements over a 15-week period. However, they were finally captured just 30 miles south of Canada's border. It was then that Chief Joseph gave this memorable speech. For the rest of his life, he petitioned for the Nez Percé people to be allowed to return to their homeland.

TEACHING SUGGESTIONS

✹ Use the Evaluate That Document! form to analyze the point of view of Chief Joseph's speech.

✹ Encourage students to practice giving the speech, and discuss the impact of hearing a speech as opposed to reading it.

✹ Let students know that Looking Glass was a famous Nez Percé warrior, and Toohulhulsote was a wise old man of the Nez Percé. Ask students to list the reasons that Chief Joseph gives for surrendering.

✹ Discuss the last line of Chief Joseph's speech, in which he surrenders. Compare the effect of his language to the simple statement, "I surrender." Discuss whether surrendering can be a more courageous act than continuing to fight.

✹ Ask students to conduct research to learn more about the history of the Nez Percé, who helped the Lewis and Clark expedition in 1805, and who attempted a peaceful coexistence with the white settlers until they were betrayed and driven from their land.

The Indian Territory: 1879

Use with pages 41–43.

BACKGROUND

In the 1830s and 1840s, 70,000 Native Americans in the Southeast were removed from their lands by the United States government and settled in the West in an area known as the Indian Territory (now Oklahoma). Their forced march was known as the Trail of Tears.

By the 1870s, the fertile land of the Indian Territory became desirable to white settlers. The advertisement on page 41 encouraging settlers to move west illustrates the climate of the time. They began encroaching, illegally, into the territory. Posters like the one shown were circulated throughout the West.

The print called "Killing Buffalo for Pleasure" on page 42 shows another aspect of the impact of the white settlers on the Native Americans' way of life. The advent of the railroad had divided herds and brought in hunters. These hunters killed buffalo for sport and also to sell their hides for profit. But another, even more insidious, motive existed—to destroy the food supply for the Native Americans and make their land available for cattle drives and settlers.

The photograph of dead buffalo on page 42 conveys the scope of the decimation of the Native Americans' way of life. The final two photographs (page 43) show Native American groups forced to live in captivity.

TEACHING SUGGESTIONS

※ Encourage students to use the Evaluate That Document! form (page 15) to analyze the different types of primary sources on pages 41–43 showing the effect of the Westward Movement on Native Americans.

※ Have students analyze the "Grand Rush for the Indian Territory!" advertisement (page 41). What point of view does it reflect about the land? Whose point of view is represented?

※ The two images on page 42 show the killing of buffalo. The engraving at the top portrays killing as a sport. The photograph shows actual buffalo lying dead. Ask students to talk about the impact of each document. Have them discuss the ways in which the slaughter of the buffalo population affected Native Americans.

※ Following this discussion, students might research why buffalo were so important to Native Americans in the Indian Territory of the United States. Tell students that by 1883 the once plentiful buffalo herds had almost vanished. Piles of buffalo skeletons were shipped to the East Coast and made into fertilizer. Ask students to research and make a chart or a map showing the shrinking buffalo population in North America during the 1800s.

※ The photographs on page 43 show Native Americans who were forced to live in captivity. Ask students to explore the expressions on their faces, their postures, and their clothing. Ask them also to examine the bearing of the captors.

※ Ask students to explore the terms *Westward Movement* and *expansion* from the perspective of Native Americans.

Evaluate That Document!

Title or name of document _____

Date of document _____

Type of document:

❏ letter   ❏ patent

❏ diary/journal   ❏ poster

❏ newspaper article   ❏ advertisement

❏ photograph   ❏ drawing/painting

❏ map   ❏ cartoon

❏ telegram   ❏ other _____

Point of view:

Who created this document? _____

For whom was this document created? _____
_____

What was the purpose for creating this document? _____
_____

What might the person who created it have been trying to express? _____
_____

What are two things you can learn about the time period from this primary source?
_____
_____

What other questions do you have about this source?

_____
_____
_____
_____
_____

The Louisiana Purchase

1803

Treaty

Between the United States of America and the French Republic

National Archives

The President of the United States of America, and the First Consul of the French Republic in the name of the French People . . . have respectively named their Plenipotentiaries to wit the President of the United States, by and with the advice and consent of the Senate of the said States; Robert R. Livingston Minister Plenipotentiary of the United States and James Monroe Minister Plenipotentiary and Envoy extraordinary of the said States near the Government of the French Republic; And the First Consul in the name of the French people, Citizen Francis Barbe Marbois Minister of the public treasury who after having respectively exchanged their full powers, have agreed to the following Articles.—

The Louisiana Purchase Treaty

Article I

Whereas by the Article the third of the Treaty concluded at St. Idelfonso the {9th Vendemiaire an 9 1st October 1800} between the First Consul of the French Republic and his Catholic Majesty it was agreed as follows.—

"His Catholic Majesty promises and engages on his part to cede to "the French Republic six months after the full and entire execution "of the conditions and stipulations herein relative to his Royal Highness the Duke of Parma, the Colony or Province of Louisiana with "the same extent that it now has in the hands of Spain, & that it had "when France possessed it; and such as it should be after the Treaties subsequently entered into between Spain and other States."

. . . And whereas in pursuance of the Treaty and particularly of the third article the French Republic has an incontestable title to the domain and to the possession of the said Territory—The First Consul of the French Republic desiring to give to the United States a strong proof of his friendship doth hereby cede to the said United States in the name of the French Republic forever and in full sovereignty the said territory with all its rights and appurtenances as fully and in the same manner as they have been acquired by the French Republic in virtue of the above mentioned Treaty concluded with his Catholic Majesty.

Art: II

In the cession made by the preceding article are included the adjacent Islands belonging to Louisiana all public lots and squares, vacant lands and all public buildings, fortifications, barracks and other edifices which are not private property. The Archives, papers and documents relative to the domain and sovereignty of Louisiana and its dependencies will be left in the possession of the Commissaries of the United States, and copies will be afterwards given in due form to the Magistrates and Municipal officers of such of the said papers and documents as may be necessary to them.

Art: III

The inhabitants of the ceded territory shall be incorporated in the Union of the United States and admitted as soon as possible according to the principles of the Federal Constitution to the enjoyment of all the rights, advantages and immunities of citizens of the United States; and in the mean time they shall be maintained and protected in the free enjoyment of their liberty, property and the Religion which they profess.

Art: IV

There shall be sent by the Government of France a Commissary to Louisiana to the end that he do every act necessary as well to receive from the Officers of his Catholic Majesty the said country and its dependencies in the name of the French Republic if it has not been already done as to transmit it in the name of the French Republic to the Commissary or agent of the United States.

The Lewis and Clark Expedition

Northwind Picture Archives

1804–1806

August 12, 1805

*We fell in with a large and plain Indian road, which came into the cove from the northeast and led along the foot of the mountains to the southwest, **obliquely** approaching the main stream, which we had left yesterday. This road we now pursued to the southwest. At 5 miles it passed a stout stream which is a principal fork of the main stream and falls into it just above the narrow pass between the two cliffs before mentioned, which we now saw below us. Here we halted and breakfasted on the last of our **venison,** having yet a small piece of pork in reserve. After eating, we continued our route through the low bottom of the main stream along the foot of the mountains on our right. The valley for 5 miles farther in a southwest direction was from 2 to 3 miles wide.*

*At the distance of 4 miles further, the road took us to the most distant fountain of the waters of the mighty Missouri in search of which we have spent so many **toilsome** days and restless nights. Thus far I had accomplished one of those great objects on which my mind has been unalterably fixed for many years. Judge, then, of the pleasure I felt in **allaying** my thirst with this pure and ice-cold water which issues from the base of a low mountain or hill of a gentle ascent for 1/2 a mile.... Two miles below, McNeal had exultingly stood with a foot on each side of this little rivulet and thanked his God that he had lived to bestride the mighty, and heretofore deemed endless, Missouri.*

After refreshing ourselves, we proceeded on to the top of the dividing ridge, from which I discovered immense ranges of high mountains still to the west of us, with their tops partially covered with snow. I now descended the mountain about 3/4 of a mile, which I found much steeper than on the opposite side, to a handsome bold running creek of cold, clear water. Here I first tasted the water of the great Columbia River.

Excerpt from *The Journals of the Expedition under the Command of Captains Lewis and Clark*

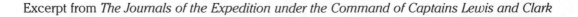

Scholastic Professional Books

The Lewis and Clark Expedition

Invoice of articles from Fort Mandan to President Thomas Jefferson

*First box: skins of the male and female antelope, with their skeletons;…
horns and ears of the black tail, or mule deer;… skeletons of this small, or burrowing wolf
of the prairies, the skin having been lost by accident.*

Second box: four buffalo robes and an ear of Mandan corn.

*Third box: skins of the male and female
antelope, with their skeletons.*

*Fourth box: specimens of earths, salts
and minerals; specimens of plants;…
one tin box containing insects.*

*In a large trunk: one buffalo robe painted
by a Mandan man representing a battle
which was fought eight years [ago],
by the Sioux and [Arikaras]
against the Mandans and [Hidastas].*

*One cage, containing four
living magpies.*

*One cage, containing a living burrowing
squirrel of the prairies.*

One cage, containing one living hen of the prairies.

One large pair of elk's horns, connected by the frontal bone.

Peabody Museum, Harvard University

1804–1805

The Lewis and Clark Expedition

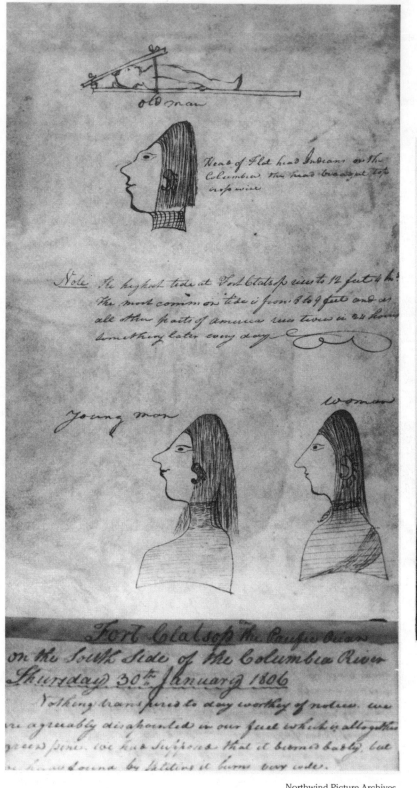

1806

c. 1804–1805

Scholastic Professional Books

The Crockett Almanac

A Desperate Contest with a Great Black Bear.

c. 1804–1805

1841

On the Trail

A Pioneer Train Constitution 1849

We the undersigned, being desirous of forming ourselves into a company for the purpose of emigrating to the Sacramento Valley in California and believing that order, good conduct, and mutual support will more effectually enable us to . . . reach our destination, we hereby bind ourselves . . . to submit to all the rules and regulations herein.

We agree:

National Archives

- *That every wagon must have been approved by the Inspector appointed and must also be provided with a team, provision, arms, and ammunition.*

- *This Company shall be known by the name of the Sacramento Company and shall consist of not exceeding fifty teams.*

- *There shall be a Colonel and Adjutant who shall be elected by the Company, . . . and there shall be five Captains.*

- *Each of the above officers [may] be removed at any time by a majority of their electors.*

- *It shall be the duty of the Colonel to have full command as a military officer . . . to superintend all for the good order of said Company.*

- *The Adjutant shall act as secretary [and] keep a roll of every man's name in said Company.*

- *The duty of the Captains will be to take command of the guard each night in rotation.*

- *Every man attached to the Company except foresaid officers must keep guard or perform other duties according to his regular turn on the roll . . . And if any be sick his or their names must be supplied by the next name or names in order on the roll.*

- *The officers of the Company shall compose a court for the trial of offenses and . . . punishments awarded according to the offense committed.*

- *Drunkenness, sleeping on guard, and neglect of orders received from the Officers to be considered grievous offenses subjecting persons convicted to . . . expulsion.*

- *All quarreling and fighting shall be considered a violation of the rules and regulations of the Company.*

- *In case of any wagon being disabled and not being able to be repaired or any team being disabled . . . the board of officers shall make such distribution of the load of said wagon among the other wagons.*

- *In case of the death of any member of the Company, an inventory of his effects shall be taken [and] said effects [distributed] to the friends or heirs.*

Scholastic Professional Books

On the Trail

c. 1850

Nebraska State Historical Society

May 21, 1849

We have a cooking stove made of sheet iron, a portable table, tin plates and cups, cheap knives and forks (best ones packed away), camp stools, etc. We sleep in our wagons on feather beds … We live on bacon, ham, rice, dried fruits, molasses, packed butter, bread, coffee, tea, and milk, as we have our own cows.

July 2, 1849

Passed Independence Rock. This rock is covered with names. With great difficulty, I found a place to cut mine. Twelve miles from this is Devil's Gate. It's an opening in the mountain through which the Sweetwater River flows. Several of us climbed this mountain—somewhat perilous for youngsters not over fourteen. … We were gone so long that the train was stopped and men sent out in search of us. We made all sorts of promises to remain in sight in the future.

Sallie Hester, 14 years old

April 23, 1847

Made nineteen miles; traveled until dark. Ate a cold bite and went to bed chilly and cold, which is very disagreeable with a parcel of little children.

April 25, 1847

Last night our cattle ran off, consequently we only made eleven miles.

June 23, 1847

At present there is one hundred and forty persons in our company. We see thousands of buffalo and have to use their dung for fuel. A man will gather a bushel in a minute; three bushels makes a good fire. We call the stuff "buffalo chips."

Elizabeth Dixon Smith, 39 years old

On the Trail

Library of Congress

The first of April came—1852. Three long lines of covered wagons, so clean and shine, but oh so battered, torn and dirty afterward. The loud callings and hilarity: many came to see us off. We took a last look at our dear homestead as it faded from our view. We crossed the Illinois River on a ferry. We looked back and saw our old watch dog (his name was Watch) howling on the distant shore....

My mother kept the two youngest with her always in "Mother's wagon." Her health was not very good, and she had dreads and fears, but hoped she would live to get to Oregon. Fate willed it otherwise, and being frail and weary with the long journey, she fell a victim to the cholera, so prevalent that year on the plains, leaving her sorrowing family to grieve for her.... We had to journey on, and leave her in a lonely grave.... Her grave is lost. No one was ever able to find it again.

Harriet Scott Palmer, looking back on her trip, made when she was 11 years old

The Gold Rush

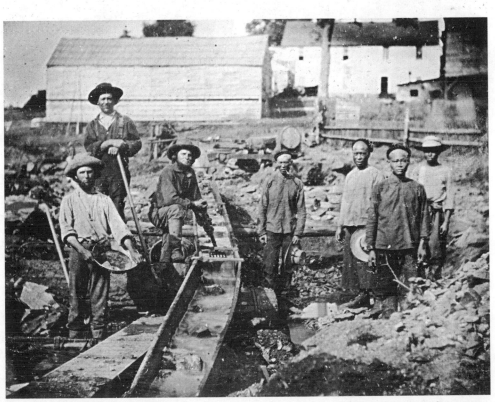

c. 1849

The Huntington Library

1852

California State Library, Sacramento

The Gold Rush

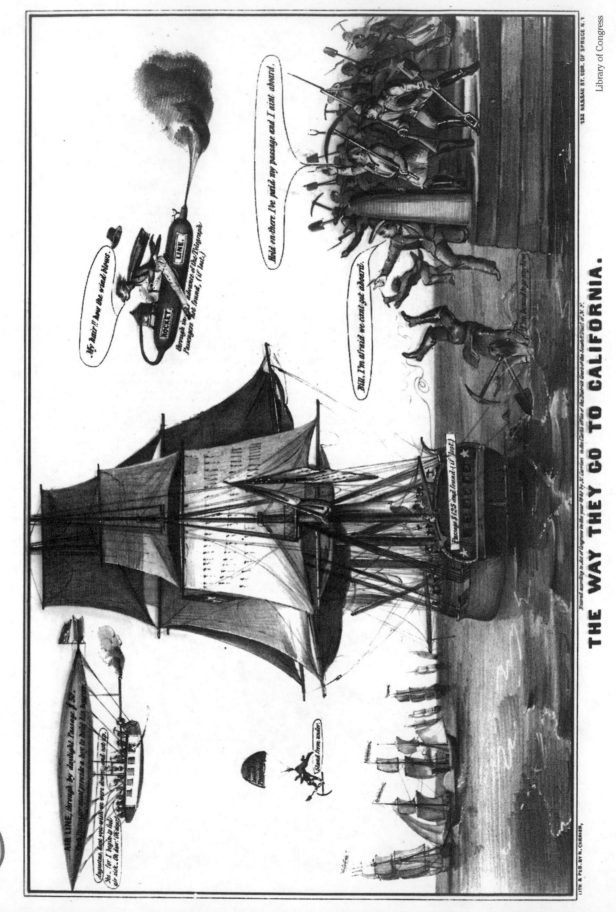

Horse Tracks

THE

PRAIRIE TRAVELER,

A HAND-BOOK

FOR

OVERLAND EXPEDITIONS.

WITH ILLUSTRATIONS, AND ITINERARIES OF
THE PRINCIPAL ROUTES BETWEEN THE
MISSISSIPPI AND THE PACIFIC,
AND A MAP.

By RANDOLPH B. MARCY,

CAPTAIN U. S. ARMY.

(NOW GENERAL MARCY, CHIEF OF STAFF, ARMY OF THE POTOMAC.)

EDITED (WITH NOTES) BY

RICHARD F. BURTON, F.R.G.S.,

ETC.

PUBLISHED IN THE UNITED STATES BY AUTHORITY OF THE WAR DEPARTMENT.

LONDON:
TRÜBNER AND CO., 60, PATERNOSTER ROW.
1863.

Denver Public Library

I have in the following cut represented the prints made by the hoofs at the ordinary speed of the walk, trot, and gallop, so that persons, in following the trail of Indians, may form an idea as to the probability of overtaking them, and regulate their movements accordingly.

Excerpt from Randolph B. Marcy's
*The Prairie Traveler, A Hand-Book for
Overland Expeditions,* 1863

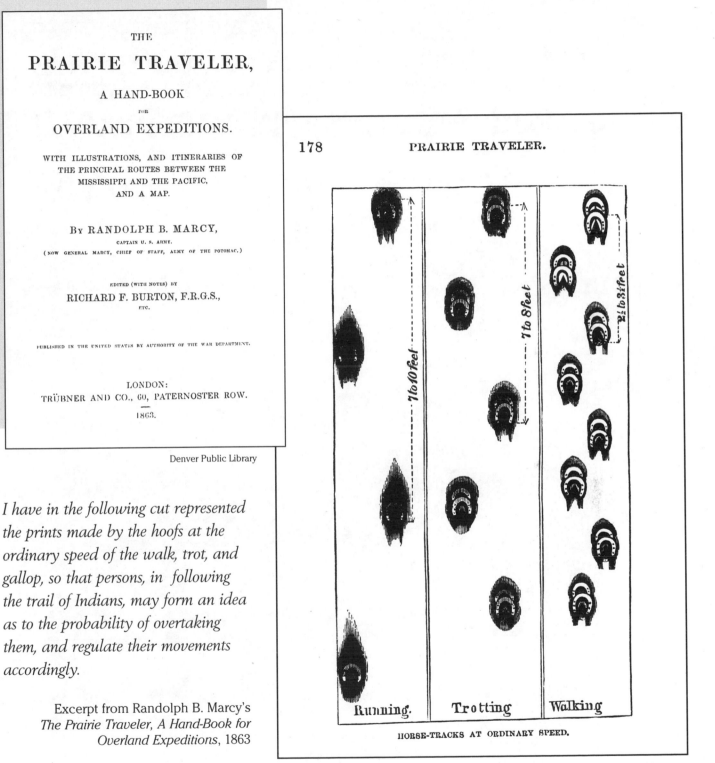

178   PRAIRIE TRAVELER.

7 to 10 feet   7 to 8 feet   2½ to 3 feet

Running.   Trotting   Walking

HORSE-TRACKS AT ORDINARY SPEED.

Library of Congress

The Pony Express

1860

Scholastic Professional Books

The Telegraph

1861

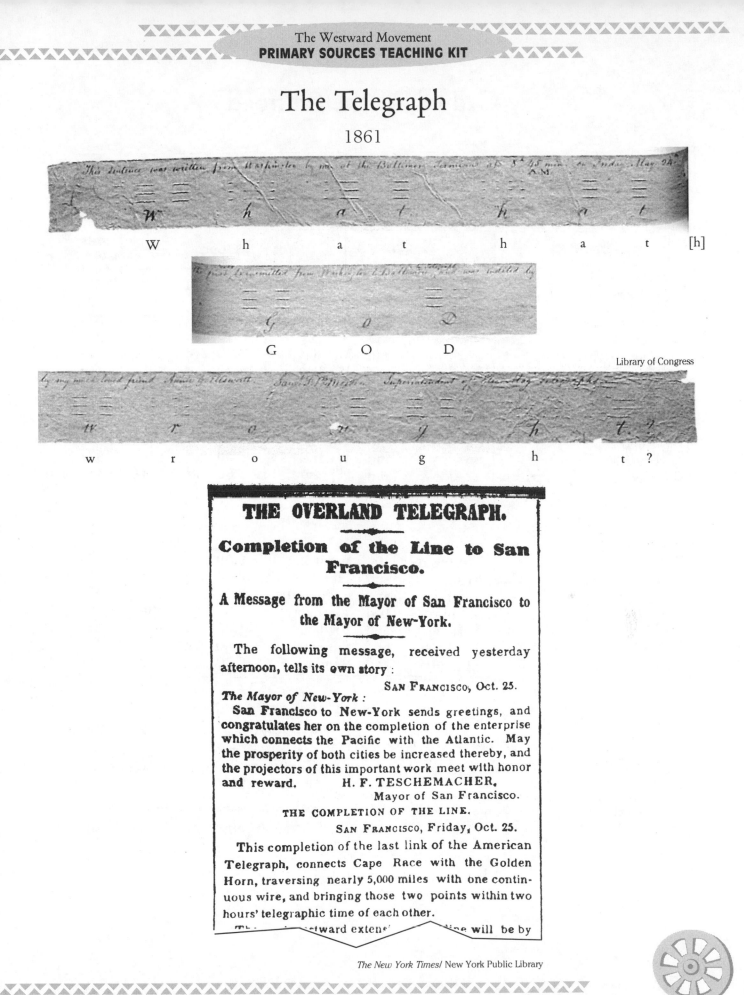

W h a t h a t [h]

G O D

w r o u g h t ?

Library of Congress

THE OVERLAND TELEGRAPH.

Completion of the Line to San Francisco.

A Message from the Mayor of San Francisco to the Mayor of New-York.

The following message, received yesterday afternoon, tells its own story :

SAN FRANCISCO, Oct. 25.

The Mayor of New-York :

San Francisco to New-York sends greetings, and congratulates her on the completion of the enterprise which connects the Pacific with the Atlantic. May the prosperity of both cities be increased thereby, and the projectors of this important work meet with honor and reward. H. F. TESCHEMACHER,

Mayor of San Francisco.

THE COMPLETION OF THE LINE.

SAN FRANCISCO, Friday, Oct. 25.

This completion of the last link of the American Telegraph, connects Cape Race with the Golden Horn, traversing nearly 5,000 miles with one continuous wire, and bringing those two points within two hours' telegraphic time of each other.

Th......westward extens........ine will be by

The New York Times/ New York Public Library

Growth of the Railroad

No. 2.	GOING WEST.				Jan. 1859.
LEAVE.	**DAYS.**		**Hour.**	**Distance, Place to Place.**	**TIME ALLOWED**
				Miles.	No. Hours.
St. Louis, Mo., and Memphis, Tenn.,	Monday	and Thursday,	8.00 A.M		
Tipton, Mo.	Monday	and Thursday,	6.00 P.M	160	10
Springfield, "	Wednesday	and Saturday,	7.45 A.M	143	37¾
Fayetteville, Ark.	Thursday	and Sunday,	10 15 A.M	100	26½
Fort Smith, "	Friday	and Monday,	3.30 A.M	65	17¼
Sherman, Texas.	Sunday	and Wednesday,	12.30 A.M	205	45
Fort Belknap, "	Monday	and Thursday,	9.00 A.M	146½	32½
Fort Chadbourne, "	Tuesday	and Friday,	3.15 P.M	136	30¼
Pecos River Crossing,	Thursday	and Sunday,	3.45 A.M	165	36½
El Paso,	Saturday	and Tuesday,	11.00 A.M	248½	55¼
Soldier's Farewell,	Sunday	and Wednesday,	8.30 P.M	150	33½
Tucson, Arizona	Tuesday	and Friday,	1.30 P.M	184½	41
Gila River,* "	Wednesday	and Saturday,	9.00 P.M	141	31½
Fort Yuma, Cal.	Friday	and Monday,	3.00 A.M	135	30
Los Angelos, "	Sunday	and Wednesday,	8.30 A.M	254	53½
Fort Tejon, "	Monday	and Thursday,	7.30 A.M	96	23
Visalia, "	Tuesday	and Friday,	11.30 A.M	127	28
Firebaugh's Ferry, "	Wednesday	and Saturday,	5.30 A.M	82	18
(Arrive) San Francisco,	Thursday	and Sunday,	8.30 A.M	163	27

* The Station referred to on the Gila River is 40 miles west of the Maricopa Wells.

This Schedule may not be exact—all employes are directed to use every possible exertion to get the Stage through in quick time, even though ahead of this time.

No allowance is made in the time for ferries, changing teams, &c. It is necessary that each driver increase his speed over the average per hour enough to gain time for meals, changing teams, crossing ferries, &c.

Every person in the Company's employ will remember that each minute is of importance. If each driver on the route loses 15 minutes, it would make a total loss of time, on the entire route, of 25 hours, or, more than one day. If each one loses 10 minutes, it would make a loss of 16½ hours, or the best part of a day.

If each driver gains that time, it leaves a margin against accidents and extra delays.

All will see the necessity of promptness; every minute of time is valuable, as the Company are under heavy forfeit if the mail is behind time.

JOHN BUTTERFIELD, President.

1859

The Huntington Library

Growth of the Railroad

Library of Congress

1869

The Golden Spike/Stanford University

*May God continue the unity of our Country as this Railroad
unites the two great Oceans of the World.*

Growth of the Railroad

1869

American Progress

1872

American Progress, 1872
by John Gast

Glidden's Barbed Wire Patent

UNITED STATES PATENT OFFICE.

JOSEPH F. GLIDDEN, OF DE KALB, ILLINOIS.

IMPROVEMENT IN WIRE FENCES.

Specification forming part of Letters Patent No. **157,124**, dated November 24, 1874; application filed October 27, 1873.

To all whom it may concern:

Be it known that I, JOSEPH F. GLIDDEN, of De Kalb, in the county of De Kalb and State of Illinois, have invented a new and valuable Improvement in Wire Fences; and that the following is a full, clear, and exact description of the construction and operation of the same, reference being had to the accompanying drawings, in which—

Figure 1 represents a side view of a section of fence exhibiting my invention. Fig. 2 is a sectional view, and Fig. 3 is a perspective view, of the same.

This invention has relation to means for preventing cattle from breaking through wire fences; and it consists in combining, with the twisted fence-wires, a short transverse wire, coiled or bent at its central portion about one of the wire strands of the twist, with its free ends projecting in opposite directions, the other wire strand serving to bind the spur-wire firmly to its place, and in position, with its spur ends perpendicular to the direction of the fence-wire, lateral movement, as well as vibration, being prevented. It also consists in the construction and novel arrangement, in connection with such a twisted fence-wire, and its spur-wires, connected and arranged as above described, of a twisting-key or head-piece passing through the fence-post, carrying the ends of the fence-wires, and serving, when the spurs become loose, to tighten the twist of the wires, and thus render them rigid and firm in position.

In the accompanying drawings, the letter B designates the fence-posts, the twisted fence-wire connecting the same being indicated by the letter A. C represents the twisting-key, the shank of which passes through the fence-post, and is provided at its end with an eye, b, to which the fence-wire is attached. The outer end of said key is provided with a transverse thumb-piece, c, which serves for its manipulation, and at the same time, abutting against the post, forms a shoulder or stop, which prevents the contraction of the wire from drawing the key through its perforation in said post.

The fence-wire is composed at least of two strands, a and z, which are designed to be twisted together after the spur-wires have been arranged in place.

The letter D indicates the spur-wires. Each of these is formed of a short piece of wire, which is bent at its middle portion, as at E, around one only of the wire strands, this strand being designated by the letter a. In forming this middle bend or coil several turns are taken in the wire, so that it will extend along the strand-wire for a distance several times the breadth of its diameter, and thereby form a solid and substantial bearing-head for the spurs, which will effectually prevent them from vibrating laterally or being pushed down by cattle against the fence-wire. Although these spur-wires may be turned at once around the wire strand, it is preferred to form the central bend first, and to then x them on the wire strand, arranging them at suitable distances apart. The spurs having thus been arranged on one of the wire strands are fixed in position and place by approaching the other wire strands z on the side of the bend from which the spurs extend, and then twisting the two strands a z together by means of the wire key above mentioned, or otherwise. This operation locks each spur-wire at its allotted place, and prevents it from moving therefrom in either direction. It clamps the bend of the spur-wire upon the wire a, thereby holding it against rotary vibration. Finally, the spur ends extending out between the strands on each side, and where the wires are more closely approximated in the twist, form shoulders or stops s, which effectually prevent such rotation in either direction.

Should the spurs, from the untwisting of the strands, become loose and easily movable on their bearings, a few turns of the twisting-key will make them firm, besides straightening up the fence-wire.

What I claim as my invention, and desire to secure by Letters Patent, is—

A twisted fence-wire having the transverse spur-wire D bent at its middle portion about one of the wire strands a of said fence-wire, and clamped in position and place by the other wire strand z, twisted upon its fellow, substantially as specified.

JOSEPH F. GLIDDEN.

Witnesses:
  G. L. CHAPIN,
  J. H. ELLIOTT.

National Archives

1873

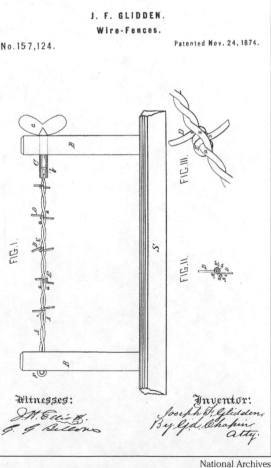

J. F. GLIDDEN.
Wire-Fences.

No. 157,124.

Patented Nov. 24, 1874.

FIG. I.

FIG. II.

FIG. III.

Witnesses:
J. W. Ellis
G. G. Billons

Inventor:
Joseph F. Glidden
By G. L. Chapin
Atty.

National Archives

Scholastic Professional Books

Life on the Frontier—Pioneers

late 1800s

Library of Congress

California Homesteader—receiving patent to land

late 1800s

Library of Congress

Life on the Frontier—Cowboys

Library of Congress

late 1800s

Library of Congress

late 1800s

Scholastic Professional Books

Life on the Frontier—Cowboys

late 1800s

Kansas State Historical Society

XIT Cowboys, members of a Texas trail-herd crew, 1890

Montana Historical Society

Scholastic Professional Books

The Wild West

c. 1898

Chief Joseph's Speech

Superstock Images

I am tired of fighting. Our chiefs are killed. Looking Glass is
dead. Toohulhulsote is dead. The old men are all dead. It is the
young men who say yes or no. He who led the young men is dead. It
is cold and we have no blankets. The little children are freezing
to death. My people, some of them, have run away to the hills, and
have no blankets, no food; no one knows where they are—perhaps
freezing to death. I want to have time to look for my children and
see how many of them I can find. Maybe I shall find them among the
dead. Hear me, my chiefs, I am tired; my heart is sick and sad.
From where the sun now stands I will fight no more forever.

Chief Joseph's surrender speech, 1877

Scholastic Professional Books

The Indian Territory

GRAND RUSH

FOR THE

INDIAN

TERRITORY !

Over 15,000,000 Acres of Land

NOW OPEN FOR SETTLEMENT !

Being part of the Land bought by the Government in 1866 from the Indians for the Freedmen.

NOW IS THE CHANCE

TO

PROCURE A HOME

In this Beautiful Country!

THE FINEST TIMBER !
THE RICHEST LAND !
THE FINEST WATERED !

WEST OF THE MISSISSIPPI RIVER.

Every person over 21 years of age is entitled to 160 acres, either by pre-emption or homestead, who wishes to settle in the Indian Territory. It is estimated that over Fifty Thousand will move to this Territory in the next ninety days. The Indians are rejoicing to have the whites settle up this country.

The Grand Expedition will Leave Independence May 7, 1879

Independence is situated at the terminus of the Kansas City, Lawrence & Southern Railroad. The citizens of Independence have laid out and made a splendid road to these lands; and they are prepared to furnish emigrants with complete outfits, such as wagons, agricultural implements, dry goods, groceries, lumber and stock. They have also opened an office there for general information to those wishing to go to the Territory. IT COSTS NOTHING TO BECOME A MEMBER OF THIS COLONY.

Persons passing through Kansas City will apply at the office of K. C. L. & S. R. R., opposite Union Depot, for Tickets.

ABOUT THE LANDS.

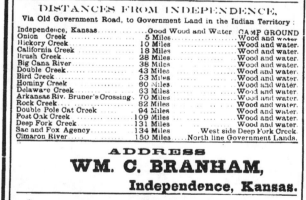

ABOUT THE LANDS.

In answer to inquiries concerning these government lands in the Indian Territory, Col. E. C. Boudinot sends the following from Washington :

FIRST—In reply I will say that the United States, by treaties made in 1866, purchased from Indian tribes, in the Indian Territory, about 14,000,000 acres of land.

SECOND—These lands were bought from the Creeks, Seminoles, Choctaws and Chickasaws, by their treaty of 1866.

The Creeks, by their treaty of 1866, sold to the United States 3,250,560 acres, for the sum of $975,168. The Seminoles, by their treaty of 1866, sold to the United States 2,169,080 acres, for the sum of $325,362.

The Choctaws and Chickasaws, by their treaty of 1866, sold to the United States the "leased lands" lying west of 98 degrees of west longitude, for the sum of $300,000. The number of acres in this tract is not specified in the treaty, but it contains about 7,000,000 acres. See 14th vol. Statutes at Large, pages 755, 769 and 786.

Of these ceded lands the United States has since appropriated for the use of the Sac and Foxes 479,567 acres and for the Pottawatomies 575,877 acres, making a total of 1,055,542 acres. These Indians occupy these lands by virtue of treaties and acts of Congress. By an unratified agreement, the Wichita Indians are now occupying 743,610 acres of these ceded lands. I presume some action will be taken by the United States government to permanently locate the Wichitas upon the land they now occupy. The title, however, to these lands is still in the United States.

By executive order, Kiowa, Comanche, Arrapahoe, and other wild Indians, have been brought upon a portion of the ceded lands, but such lands are a part of the public domain of the United States, and have all been surveyed and sectionised.

A portion of these 14,000,000 acres of land, however, has not been appropriated by the United States for the use of other Indians and all probability never will be.

THIRD.—These unappropriated lands are situated immediately west of the 97th degree of west longitude and south of the Cherokee territory. The soil is well adapted for the production of corn, wheat and other cereals. Is is unsurpassed for grazing, and is well watered and timbered.

FOURTH.—The United States have an absolute and unembarrassed title to every acre of these 14,000,000 acres, unless it be to the 1,054,544 now occupied by the Sac and Fox and Pottawatomie Indians. The Indian title has been extinguished. The articles of the treaties with the Creeks and Seminoles, by which they sold their lands, begin with the statement that the lands are ceded "in compliance with the desire of the United States to locate other Indians and freedmen thereon." By the express terms of these treaties the lands bought by the United States were not intended for the exclusive use of other Indians" as has been so often asserted. They were bought as much for the negroes of the country as for Indians.

DISTANCES FROM INDEPENDENCE.

Via Old Government Road, to Government Land in the Indian Territory :

Independence, Kansas	Good Wood and Water	CAMP GROUND
Onion Creek	5 Miles	Wood and water.
Hickory Creek	10 Miles	Wood and water.
California Creek	18 Miles	Wood and water.
Brush Creek	28 Miles	Wood and water.
Big Cana River	38 Miles	Wood and water.
Double Creek	43 Miles	Wood and water.
Bird Creek	53 Miles	Wood and water.
Hominy Creek	60 Miles	Wood and water.
Delaware Creek	63 Miles	Wood and water.
Arkansas Riv. Bruner's Crossing	70 Miles	Wood and water.
Rock Creek	82 Miles	Wood and water.
Double Pole Cat Creek	94 Miles	Wood and water.
Post Oak Creek	109 Miles	Wood and water.
Deep Fork Creek	131 Miles	Wood and water.
Sac and Fox Agency	134 Miles	West side Deep Fork Creek.
Cimaron River	150 Miles	North line Government Lands.

ADDRESS
WM. C. BRANHAM,
Independence, Kansas.

To parties accompanying my Colony, I would advise them to purchase their Outfit at Independence, Kas. I have examined Stock and Prices of Goods, such as Wagons, Plows, Lumber, Dry Goods, Groceries, and, in fact, everything that is needed by Parties settling upon new Land, and find them as cheap as they can be bought in the East.

RESPECTFULLY YOURS,
Col. C. C. CARPENTER.

P. S. Parties will have no trouble in getting transportation at Independence for buying or hauling goods in the Territory.   C. C. C.

1879

The Indian Territory

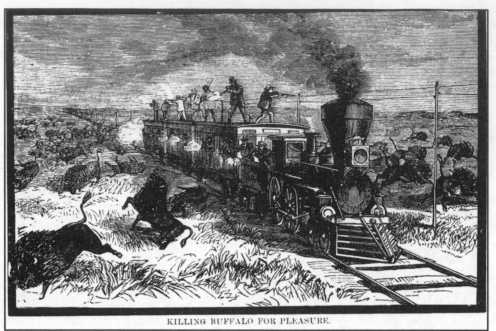

late 1800s

KILLING BUFFALO FOR PLEASURE.

Library of Congress

1880

THE HIDE HUNTER'S WORK   MONTANA 1880

Coffrin Old West Gallery

Scholastic Professional Books

The Indian Territory

late 1800s   Nebraska State Historical Society

Eight Crow prisoners under guard at Crow Agency, Missouri, 1887   National Archives

KWL Chuck Wagon Chart

In the wagon chart below, write down what you already know about the Westward Movement in the *K* box, and then what you want to learn in the *W* box. When you've found the answers to your questions, record your discoveries in the *L* box and new questions in the *What I still want to learn* section.

K *What I know*

W *What I want to know*

L *What I learned*

What I still want to learn

The Westward Movement Map (1800s)

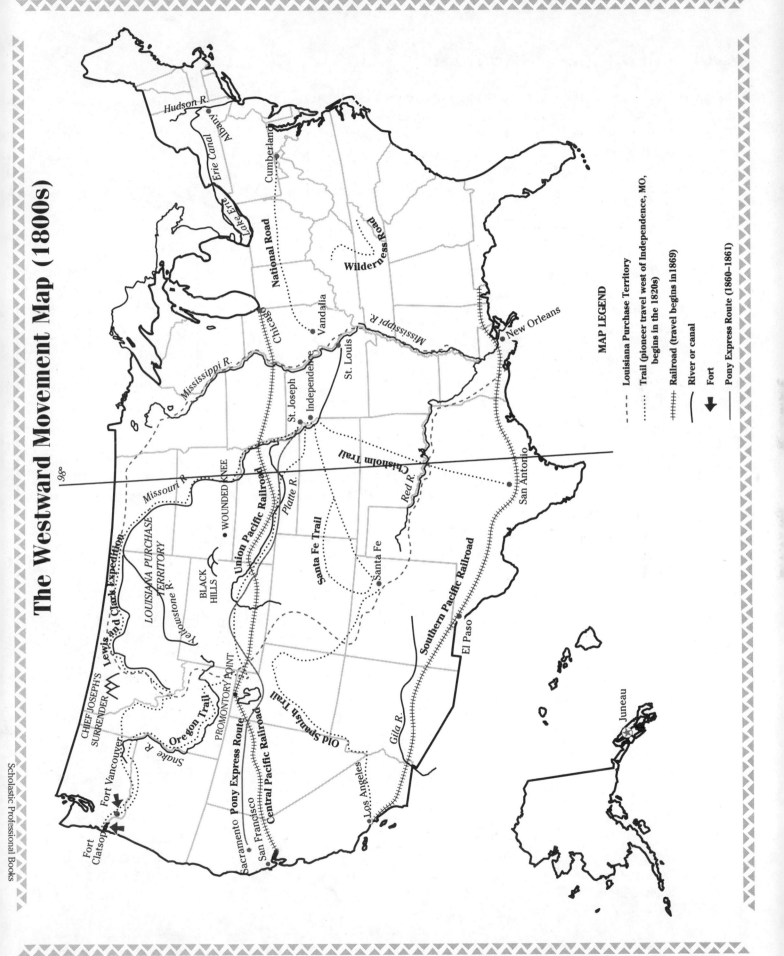

MAP LEGEND

- – – – – Louisiana Purchase Territory
- · · · · · · Trail (pioneer travel west of Independence, MO, begins in the 1820s)
- +++++ Railroad (travel begins in 1869)
- ———— River or canal
- ▼ Fort
- ——— Pony Express Route (1860–1861)

Survival on the Oregon Trail Game Cards

*L*ife on the Oregon Trail was not a game. But playing this simple game can give you an idea of some of the hardships faced by the pioneers. Make a simple game board of the Oregon Trail using the drawing below. Then cut out these game cards. Using coins as markers, take turns drawing cards and advancing to the end of the Oregon Trail.

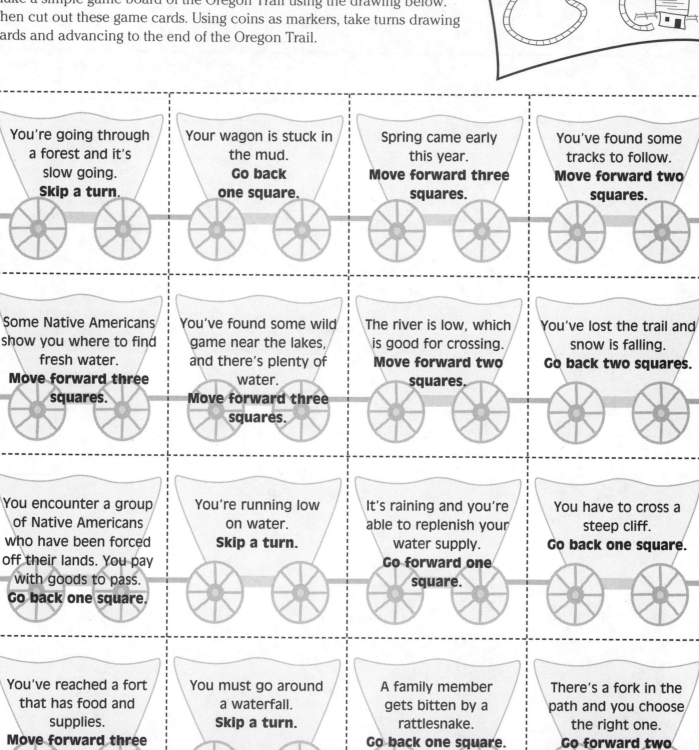

You're going through a forest and it's slow going. **Skip a turn**.

Your wagon is stuck in the mud. **Go back one square**.

Spring came early this year. **Move forward three squares.**

You've found some tracks to follow. **Move forward two squares.**

Some Native Americans show you where to find fresh water. **Move forward three squares**.

You've found some wild game near the lakes, and there's plenty of water. **Move forward three squares.**

The river is low, which is good for crossing. **Move forward two squares.**

You've lost the trail and snow is falling. **Go back two squares.**

You encounter a group of Native Americans who have been forced off their lands. You pay with goods to pass. **Go back one square.**

You're running low on water. **Skip a turn.**

It's raining and you're able to replenish your water supply. **Go forward one square**.

You have to cross a steep cliff. **Go back one square**.

You've reached a fort that has food and supplies. **Move forward three squares.**

You must go around a waterfall. **Skip a turn.**

A family member gets bitten by a rattlesnake. **Go back one square.**

There's a fork in the path and you choose the right one. **Go forward two squares.**

Crack the Code

Morse code is still used in some places as a way to communicate information in code. Use this chart to decode the words below. Then create your own Morse code message.

Morse Code

A	B	C	CH	D	E	F	G	H
.-	-...	-.-.	----	-..	.	..-.	--.	....

I	J	K	L	M	N	O	P	Q
..	.---	-.-	.-..	--	-.	---	.--.	--.-

R	S	T	U	V	W	X	Y	Z
.-.	...	-	..-	...-	.--	-..-	-.--	--..

1	2	3	4	5	6
.----	..---	...--	....-	.....	-....

7	8	9	10
--...	---..	----.	-----

Period	Comma	Colon	Question Mark	Apostrophe	Parentheses	Quotation Marks	Hyphen
.-.-.-	--..--	---...	..--..	.----.	-.--.-	.-..-.	-....-

S–O–S!   Here's how you can practice sending your own messages to a friend. Unfold a paper clip. Staple a row of connected staples onto a piece of paper. Tap the paper clip against the staples for a dot and run the paper clip across the staples for a dash. Make sure you each have a copy of the chart in front of you!

Try to break these codes!

1.   ‑‑ ‑.‑‑ / ‑. .‑ ‑‑ . / .. ...

   _____   _____   _____

2.   .‑ ... ‑ .‑ ‑. ‑.. / ‑ ‑‑ . ‑. ‑. ‑.

   _____   _____

3.   .. ‑. ... . ‑. ‑ ...

   _____

Name _____   Date _____

The Westward Movement Glossary

During the Westward Movement, people developed phrases to describe the new life they were experiencing, on the trail, on the frontier, on the ranch, and in the West in general. Take a look at the glossary below. Then write a short story using some of these expressions.

Pioneer Talk

bonanza
a sudden windfall; from the Spanish *bonanza*, meaning success

bronco
a wild horse; from the Spanish *bronco*

chaps
leg coverings made from leather, worn by cowboys; from the Spanish *chaparajos*

chuck wagon
the wagon on the cattle drive that carried all the supplies; *chuck* meant food

get a wiggle on
to hurry up (also: **pony up**)

make the grade
to reach a goal; from the railroad era, when a train needs to climb a steep grade to the top of a mountain pass

pan out
when something becomes successful; from panning for gold

put a spoke in the wheel
to deliberately mess something up

slumgullion
a stew made with any available vegetables and meat; from necessity during the California gold rush

Story Starter Tip!

If you choose to write a story about life on the trail during the Westward Movement, here are some questions to get you started:

*Who are the characters and why are they making the journey west? What do they want?

*Who will go on the journey? Who will stay behind?

*What will they pack and what might they have to leave behind?

*What trail will they take? Where will they start from?

*Which places will they rest at and gather water and supplies? What problems might they encounter along the way?

*Which will their final destination be?

Scholastic Professional Books